FULL SCORE
WSB-12-008

吹奏楽譜 ブラスロック・シリーズ
BRASS ROCK

だったん人の踊り Brass Rock

作曲：Alexander Borodin　編曲：郷間幹男

楽器編成表

Piccolo
Flutes 1（& *2）
*Oboe
*Bassoon
*E♭ Clarinet
B♭ Clarinet 1
B♭ Clarinet 2
*B♭ Clarinet 3
*Alto Clarinet
Bass Clarinet
Alto Saxophone 1
*Alto Saxophone 2
Tenor Saxophone
Baritone Saxophone

B♭ Trumpet 1
B♭ Trumpet 2
*B♭ Trumpet 3
F Horns 1（& *2）
F Horns 3（& *4）
Trombone 1
Trombone 2
*Trombone 3
Euphonium
Tuba
Electric Bass
（String Bass）

Drums

Percussion 1
...Conga, Wind Chime

Percussion 2
...Tambourine, Triangle

Percussion 3
...Sus.Cymbal, Wind Chime, Triangle

Mallet
...Glockenspiel, Xylophone

Full Score

＊イタリック表記の楽譜はオプション

Polovetsian Dances Brass Rock - 5

ご注文について

ウィンズスコアの商品は全国の楽器店、ならびに書店にてお求めになれますが、店頭でのご購入が困難な場合、当社PC&モバイルサイト・FAX・電話からのご注文で、直接ご購入が可能です。

◎当社PCサイトでのご注文方法
http://www.winds-score.com
上記のURLへアクセスし、WEBショップにてご注文ください。

◎FAXでのご注文方法
FAX.03-6809-0594
24時間、ご注文を承ります。当社サイトよりFAXご注文用紙をダウンロードし、印刷、ご記入の上ご送信ください。

◎お電話でのご注文方法
TEL.0120-713-771
営業時間内に電話いただければ、電話にてご注文を承ります。

◎モバイルサイトでのご注文方法
右のQRコードを読み取ってアクセスいただくか、URLを直接ご入力ください。

※この出版物の全部または一部を権利者に無断で複製(コピー)することは、著作権の侵害にあたり、著作権法により罰せられます。
※造本には十分注意しておりますが、万一、落丁・乱丁などの不良品がありましたらお取り替えいたします。また、ご意見・ご感想もホームページより受け付けておりますので、お気軽にお問い合わせください。

Piccolo

だったん人の踊り Brass Rock

Comp. by Alexander Borodin
Arr. by Mikio Gohma

Flutes 1&2

だったん人の踊り Brass Rock

Comp. by Alexander Borodin
Arr. by Mikio Gohma

Oboe

だったん人の踊り Brass Rock

Comp. by Alexander Borodin
Arr. by Mikio Gohma

Bassoon

だったん人の踊り Brass Rock

Comp. by Alexander Borodin
Arr. by Mikio Gohma

MEMO

MEMO

Bass Clarinet

だったん人の踊り Brass Rock

Comp. by Alexander Borodin
Arr. by Mikio Gohma

Alto Saxophone 1

だったん人の踊り Brass Rock

Comp. by Alexander Borodin
Arr. by Mikio Gohma

だったん人の踊り Brass Rock

Baritone Saxophone

Comp. by Alexander Borodin
Arr. by Mikio Gohma

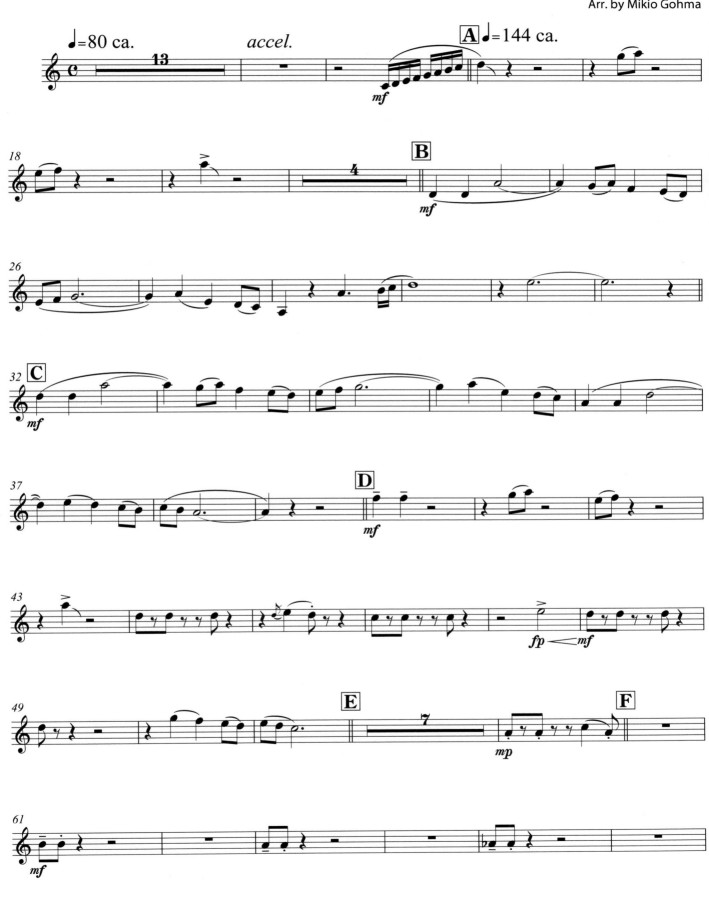

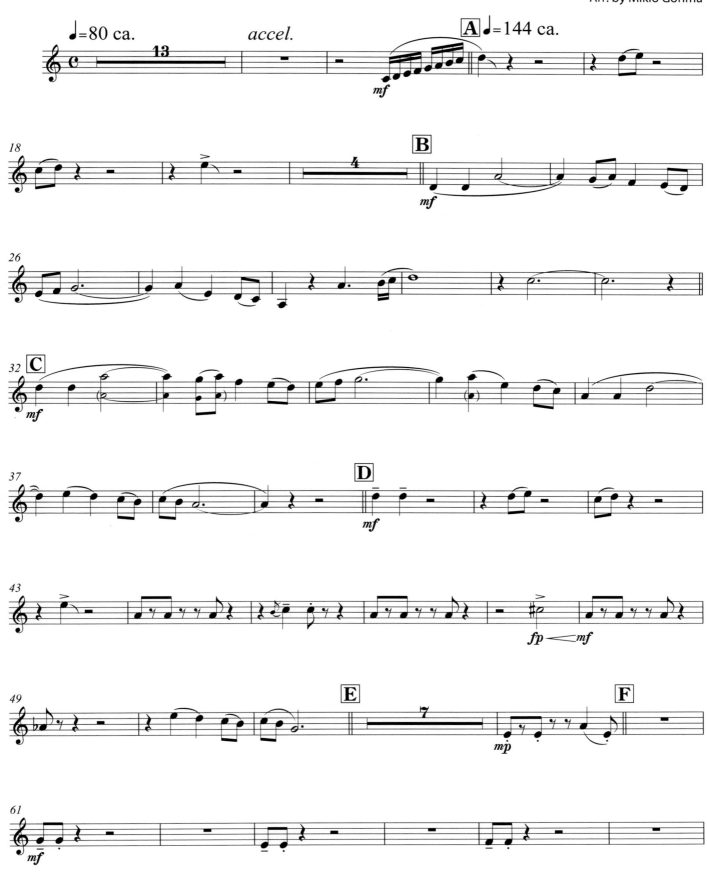

F Horns 1&2

だったん人の踊り Brass Rock

Comp. by Alexander Borodin
Arr. by Mikio Gohma

F Horns 3&4

だったん人の踊り Brass Rock

Comp. by Alexander Borodin
Arr. by Mikio Gohma

Trombone 1

だったん人の踊り Brass Rock

Comp. by Alexander Borodin
Arr. by Mikio Gohma

Trombone 2

だったん人の踊り Brass Rock

Comp. by Alexander Borodin
Arr. by Mikio Gohma

Trombone 3

だったん人の踊り Brass Rock

Comp. by Alexander Borodin
Arr. by Mikio Gohma

Tuba

だったん人の踊り Brass Rock

Comp. by Alexander Borodin
Arr. by Mikio Gohma

Electric Bass Guitar
(String Bass)

だったん人の踊り Brass Rock

Comp. by Alexander Borodin
Arr. by Mikio Gohma

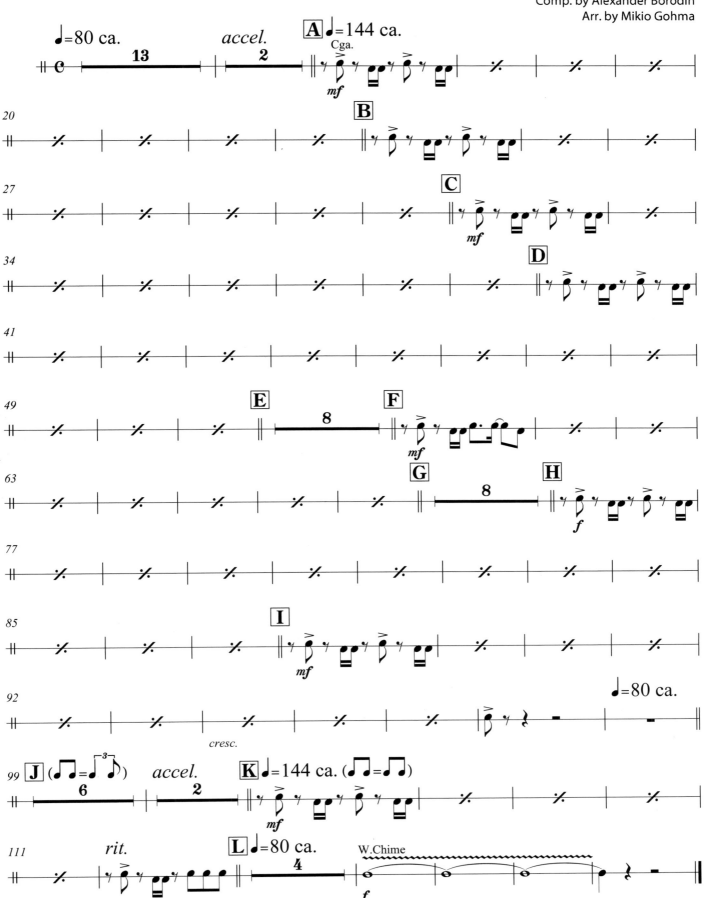

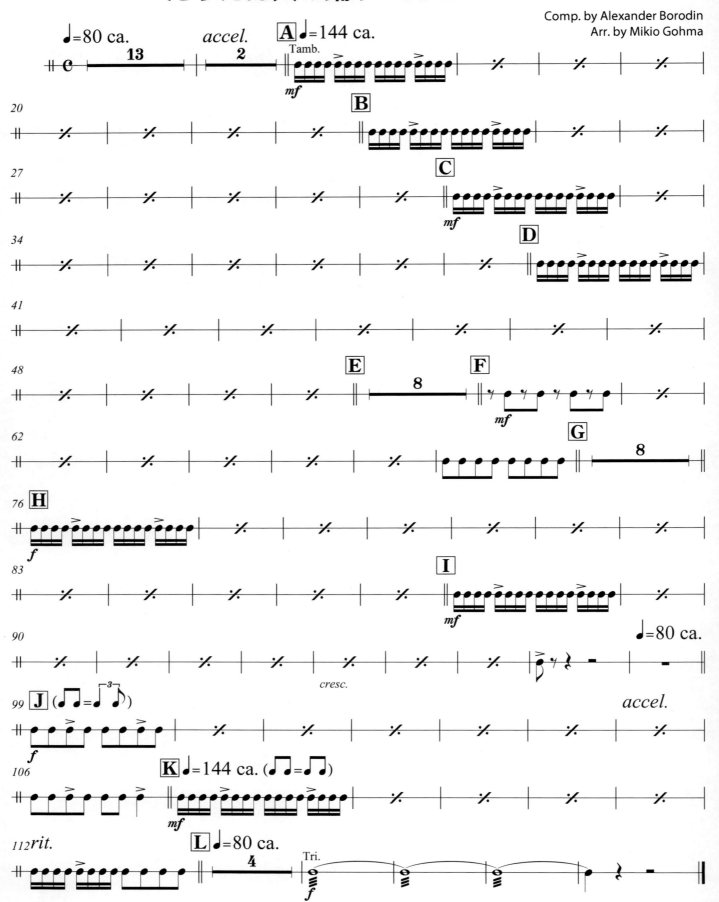

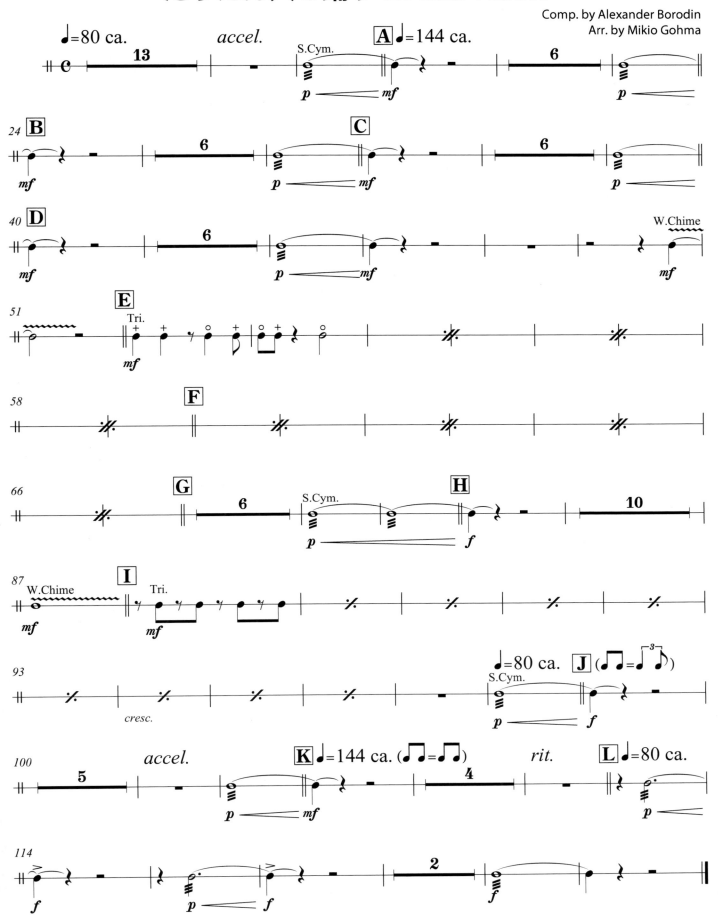